# All Hair is Good Hair

By Vontavia J. Heard

Chick Lit Publishing LLC

Copyright © 2023 by Vontavia J. Heard

All Rights Reserved.

No part of this book may be used or reproduced by any means, graphic, electronic, or mechanical, including photocopying, recording, taping, or by any information storage retrieval system without the written permission of the publisher except in the case of brief quotations embodied in critical articles and reviews.

**Dedicated to every black
girl who was ever told they
had "bad hair".**

Dear Little Black Girl,
All hair is "good hair"

Long hair, Short hair

Straight hair, Curly hair

Coily hair, Kinky hair

Big hair, Small hair

All hair is "good hair"

Wild hair, Styled hair

Slicked hair, Spiked hair

Old hair, Bold hair

Brown hair, Blue hair

All hair is "good hair"

Dear Little Black Girl,
YOUR hair is "GOOD hair"

Your hair is your crown

Whether you wear it up or down

Your hair is divine

It is one of a kind

It does not matter how you do your hair

As long as you treat it with love and care

# The End

# Dear Little Black Girl: What do you love about YOUR hair?

_____

_____

_____

_____

_____

_____

## Other books by Vontavia J. Heard

Chasing Butterflies
The Alphabet Book
Everything's NOT Okay
Love, Mr. Hedgehog

Made in the USA
Columbia, SC
17 March 2025